PULL AHEAD BOOKS

Health

Playing Safely

by Robin Nelson

Series consultants: Sonja Green, MD, and
Distinguished Professor Emerita Ann Nolte, PhD

Lerner

Lerner Books • London • New York • Minneapolis

This book was first published in the United States of America in 2006.

First published in the United Kingdom in 2008 by
Lerner Books,
Dalton House,
60 Windsor Avenue,
London SW19 2RR

Website address: www.lernerbooks.co.uk

This edition was updated and edited for UK publication by Discovery Books Ltd.,
Unit 3, 37 Watling Street, Leintwardine, Shropshire SY7 0LW

Words in **bold** type are explained in a glossary on page 31.

British Library Cataloguing in Publication Data

Nelson, Robin, 1971-

   Playing safely. - (Pull ahead books. Health)
   1. Accidents - Prevention - Juvenile literature 2. Play -
   Juvenile literature
   I. Title
   613.6

   ISBN-13: 978 1 58013 402 6

Printed in China

Peter is getting ready to ride his bike to the shops with his mum. What do they need to do to stay safe?

Peter and his mum need to wear
helmets. A helmet protects your
head if you fall.

What rules keep you safe when you are on the road? Ride close to the **curb** and be aware of cars.

Use hand signals. Signals show others where you are going.

Obey all **traffic** signs when you ride
your bike or walk. Stop when you see
a give way sign.

Cross the road only at **crossings.**

Look all ways for cars before crossing
the road. Walk your bike across busy
crossings.

There is Peter's friend Matthew.
Matthew is playing with a ball. He
waves to Peter. His ball rolls into the
road. What should Matthew do?

Stop! Never chase a ball into the road.
Ask an adult to help you get your ball.

Zack and Sarah are going to the swimming pool. Sarah is wearing rollerblades. Sarah wears a helmet and knee and wrist **pads** for protection.

Zack and Sarah can't wait to get into the pool. But they know they need to follow water safety rules.

First, Zack and Sarah put on
suncream. Suncream protects your
skin from the hot sun.

Then they make sure there is a
lifeguard. The lifeguard watches the
pool to keep everyone safe.

Walk! Don't run around a pool. You could slip and fall very easily.

Play in **shallow** water. Your feet
should be able to touch the bottom
with your head out of the water.

It is only safe to dive in deep water.
Check that it is safe before diving.

Pay attention to signs around the pool. They tell you important rules to keep you safe.

NO DIVING

Always swim with an adult nearby.

Do you know what to do in a pool emergency?

Shout for help!

Here comes the lifeguard! If no
one comes, go and find the lifeguard
or an adult.

The lifeguard is the best person to pull
the swimmer to safety. The lifeguard
has special training.

Take swimming lessons to learn more about what to do in an emergency. Swimming lessons teach you how to be safe in the water.

After lessons, Sarah's dad is waiting to drive her home. She says good-bye and fastens her seat belt. It helps her to be safe in the car.

Zack and Sarah had a great day. They remembered rules to keep them safe. They stayed safe and had fun!

What Did You Learn?

■ Wear a helmet and pads when skating or riding a bike. Use hand signals.

■ Be careful around cars and on the road. Look in all directions and obey traffic signs.

■ Wear suncream.

■ Don't run around the pool.

■ Swim and play in shallow water.

■ Don't swim without a lifeguard or an adult.

■ It is important to know what to do in a pool emergency. Here are some things to remember:
   ● call for help
   ● push something that floats, like a life jacket, out to the swimmer
   ● find the lifeguard or an adult to help
   ● don't get in the water with the swimmer.

■ When you get into a car always fasten your seat belt.

Hand Signals

When you are riding your bike you should use hand signals to show others where you are going. There are three signals.

■ Remember to look over your right shoulder to check for traffic before you start cycling. Put your right hand out to show you are going to pull out.

■ Put your left hand straight out if you are going to turn left.

■ Put your right hand straight out if you are going to turn right.

Books and Websites

Books

Pancella, Peggy. *Bicycle Safety* (Be Safe!) Heinemann, 2005.

Pancella, Peggy. *Playground Safety* (Be Safe!) Heinemann, 2005.

Pancella, Peggy. *Water Safety* (Be Safe!) Heinemann, 2005.

Royston, Angela. *Why Do Bones Break?: And Other Questions About Movement* (Body Matters) Heinemann, 2003.

Senker, Cath. *Exercise and Play* (Health Choices) Hodder Children's Books, 2007.

Websites

Hedgehogs Road Safety Website
   http://www.hedgehogs.gov.uk/main/main.html

The Children's Traffic Club
   http://www.trafficclub.org

Welltown
   http://www.welltown.gov.uk/teachers/sitemap.html

Glossary

crossings: marked paths for people crossing the road

curb: the edge of a road

helmets: hats that are worn to protect the head

lifeguard: a person who watches swimmers to keep them safe

pads: gear that protects your body if you fall

shallow: not deep

suncream: a lotion that stops sunburn

traffic: cars, lorries and buses on roads

Index